George Lansbury

J. S. J. Edwards

Published by Joyful Bertie Publishing

Copyright 2016 J. S. J. Edwards

George Lansbury Man Of Faith

J. S. J. Edwards

Introduction

From the very first time I started to read George Lansbury's story he fascinated me. His life spanned across probably the most turbulent time in recent history and at every turn and twist in the road he was there, usually long before anyone else. Heavily involved in the Suffragette's Votes For Women Movement, the Peace Campaign and social reform, primarily in the East End, Mr. Lansbury soon became prominent nationally in support of his many causes.

As I researched more thoroughly I realised just what a force for good he was, a powerhouse of a man with a voice people took notice of. GL, as he was known affectionately or "Good old George" and also "London's Fairy Godfather" gives us some idea of his popularity.

It's hard in the modern era to imagine the deprivation and destitution suffered by so many of the population, especially in the area of Bow and Bromley, but GL was one of several people who pushed for change. Perhaps Lansbury's greatest achievement was Poplarism, a cause he and his fellow councillors were prepared to spend six weeks in prison for.

Never a man to hide his feelings, he was removed from the Houses of Parliament for a verbal attack on the Prime Minister of the day over the terrible treatment of the Suffragettes in jail.

Right at the very core of George Lansbury however, was his Christian faith. Like many he wavered and fell off the path, letting his political beliefs have preference over his spiritual needs. When he returned to the fold chastened, GL served God along with his wife Bessie for the last forty years of his life as a member of Bow Church, Bow Road.

Described as a bear of a man with a ruddy complexion GL stood out in the streets of the capital city. He also favoured a distinctive mutton chop beard and was rather fond of sporting a bowler hat, so he was easily recognisable by the general public who made their feelings known to him. Usually addressing him in familiar terms as George, perfect strangers would rush up to him to say thank you for the assistance he had given to the East End community. As a non driver it was either Shank's Pony (your own two feet) or public transport that got Lansbury from A to B and on many journeys heated political discussions took place with fellow passengers. I don't think GL ever had time to switch off, for even at his home, 39 Bow Road it was open house. The scene of political gatherings and anyone down on their luck to call in hopes of help, usually of a financial nature from the generous pockets of Mr. Lansbury.

In his career which was varied to say the least, GL was a newspaper editor, author, wholesale grocer, railway contractor, van driver, cricket groundsman, stone crusher, farm labourer, mayor of Poplar, Labour Party leader, clerk, election campaign agent, secretary, Member of Parliament, chair of various bodies in support of peace, war correspondent, Poor Law Guardian, coffee house manager, Leader of the Opposition, First Commissioner of Works etc. GL was happiest in the role of being a husband and father. A big hearted man with enough love for his wife Bessie, his twelve children, his extended family, in fact enough love to embrace the entire world.

Mr. Lansbury hoped to create a Utopian society spreading out from his beloved Bow where everyone loved and helped each other. This is of course the basis of Christianity, for we are commanded to love not just our neighbour, but our neighbour's neighbour. Sadly, even a man held in such high esteem as Mr. Lansbury couldn't achieve this aim for evil has its time to rule. Like GL I know we have the next life to look forward to, a place in Heaven for those who choose the rocky path to salvation. For those people who ask the question how can you believe implicitly in something that can't be seen? Quite easily actually, it's called faith.

SECTION ONE

CONTENTS

CHAPTER ONE

The Railway Workers
George Lansbury The Son

CHAPTER TWO

Dear Mr. Lansbury
Bessie
The Poplar Workhouse

CHAPTER THREE

In The Footsteps Of George Lansbury
The Wishing Well
A Prayer For Peace And Unity

CHAPTER FOUR

Dear Mr. Lansbury We Really Need Your Help
Song For George Lansbury
George Lansbury's Silent Partner
The Battlefield

CHAPTER FIVE

Votes For Women
In The Front Room 39 Bow Road
Read All About It

CHAPTER SIX

It's Hell Here, No Lie
Power Over The Poor
Life In The East End

CHAPTER SEVEN

Giving A Voice To An East End Child
Poplarism - In Memory Of Minnie Lansbury
George Lansbury The Fighter

CHAPTER EIGHT

I Hear The Roar
Our Message
Sunday Morning
George Lansbury The Orator

CHAPTER NINE

To See George Lansbury
Saul And His Epiphany
I Pray For A New World

CHAPTER TEN

From The Wings Please Step Forward Mr. George Lansbury
Goodbye Mr. Lansbury
Looking At Modern Life From The Prospective Of GL

Rally For George Lansbury

From the platform,
I address the crowd,
With praise for George Lansbury,
I shout clear and loud,
A man of steel,
A man of stone,
Immovable,
Prepared to stand alone,
Ahead of his time,
A man of conviction,
For his beliefs,
More than once suffered prison,
Champion of women's rights,
The East End's friend,
Observed people's plight,
As a social reformer,
He put it right,
Mayor of Poplar,
He lowered the rent,
Labour leader,
A man of commitment,
A man of faith,
A rare being,
He bucked the trend,
MP for Bromley and Bow,
A pacifist to the end,
No man more worthy,
To be defined,
By the one word,
That springs to mind,
HERO.

CHAPTER ONE

George Lansbury entered this world at a house on Halesworth's High Street, Suffolk on 22nd February, 1859. There is a plaque attached to number 14 by the local historical society that confirms it.

His father, George senior was in charge of a gang of men who were constructing the railways in that area. At the time of George's birth they were track laying for a viaduct on the East Suffolk Line. It was of course by its very nature a migrant occupation, so the family moved on a regular basis.

In general railway workers were shunned by the people in the surrounding community as being beyond the pale. For most of these navvies or navigationals, to use the correct term were heavy drinkers and their use of profanities liberal.

The living conditions for these men and their families were usually very primitive, being quickly built, temporary shelters. It was this poor start that fuelled Lansbury in his later years. Having been a witness to the drunken degradation of both his parents it led to him being teetotal all his life.

It must have been incredibly hard for the Lansbury family with eventually nine children to feed and clothe. They left the pleasant town of Halesworth which was nine miles inland and travelled south to East London. It would have been a big change for young George as the area was rather gloomy and industrial, but he fell in love with the place and its people and for the rest of his life he called it home. A very lucky move for the East Enders of course and who knew then among his social circle just what a force for good he would become, a powerhouse of a man with a voice people took notice of.

George's mother, Anne Lansbury, nee Ferris was of Welsh extraction and she was a tremendous influence on his childhood. Anne was a member of a religious group called the Sabbatarians which meant that they observed Saturday as their Sabbath. She was also a radical Liberal and Anne taught her son how to read from the pages of Reynold's Newspaper. It contained articles on the reformers of the day like John Bright, William Cobden and William Ewart Gladstone. George then, along with his siblings grew up in an interesting household, on the one hand witnessing the evils of alcohol and on the other he was given the political and religious grounding that moulded his later life.

It was the National League of Education that began a campaign for free, compulsory and non-Christian education for all children. The bill was introduced and quickly passed and the Education Act of 1870 was the first piece of legislation to deal with schools. It changed the lives of so many youngsters, particularly girls who up to then had received little, if any learning. The reason being that they were expected to marry as soon as possible and large families just couldn't afford the expense. George's mother was rare at that time for being literate, and it was no doubt due to her Sabbatarianism as the various sects did teach their followers the rudiments of the three R's.

Many households could not afford much in the way of reading material other than newspapers, so they played a very important role in the day to day existence of the working class.

There was one book however, that may well have been present in the majority of homes and that was the Bible. Christianity on the whole was a much more relevant and integral part of the fabric of society. A far cry from our modern secular age where most churches have less than twenty members attending services. In fact it is a complete swing about to anyone professing Christ as Lord to be mocked and pilloried. The symbol of the cross and its meaning lost in the cult of celebrity.

Arriving in the East End was a fortuitous event for the Lansburys because their new accommodation on the London, Chatham and Dover Railway was a wooden hut, though it was still a far cry from a proper dwelling place.

As they moved along the line to Greenwich, Bethnal Green and Whitechapel things were even better as their home for a considerable time was a large Georgian house in the grounds of the Great Eastern Railway. One can only imagine the delight of George, his brothers and sisters to have a bricks and mortar house to play in for the first time in their lives. It must have taken a while to get used to stairs, multiple rooms and windows. Up to then the children would have been squashed into one bed in a corner of a shack with rudimentary facilities for washing. In today's world it is hard to believe water hasn't always been there indoors at the turn of a tap. Back in George's childhood it would have been a cold water tap outside and more than likely shared with neighbours. As were privvies, latrines, conveniences, call them what you will, all another name for a toilet. A small brick building with no sink remember, and back then they didn't flush. Wait for this at dusk men would go round with a horse and cart to empty these facilities. They were called night soil men, what a job, I can't think nowadays they would find folks willing to work under the circumstances our grandparents did.

George would have started at the age of three with simple learning and it was indeed a patchy education due to their lifestyle. Some of the schools he attended were nothing more than a single room with a lady of dubious qualification imparting the alphabet. George was made head boy by one woman, though this new rank obliged him to thread her sewing needle or unravel her wool I doubt he picked up much more than a knowledge of knit row, purl row. Instead of teaching she spent most of the school day on her hobbies.

It must have been with sighs of relief all round when George senior left the nomadic lifestyle and found a surface job at the coal mines. At last the family were settled and they were able to enjoy the novelty of lasting friendships and embrace normality.

At the age of eleven George junior was thrust out into the work force and he began his career as an office clerk. Even at that tender age he knew his own mind and could hold sway with his elders on his favourite subject which was peace. The Franco-Prussian War was under way and George with confidence way beyond his years made his views known. It didn't exactly make him very popular for Great Britain was The Empire, the fighting machine producing not only cannon fodder, but also the cannons.

After a year as a clerk George returned to school and remained at the one attached to Whitechapel Church until he was fourteen years old.

The Railway Workers

The navvies toiled, stirring up the soil,
Clothes clammy with sweat,
In cold, icy winter weather,
And beneath the summer sun blazing down,
On their bare backs,
As they laid new tracks,
Hard work, low pay,
But it didn't stop them drinking it away,
No food on the table, but dry bread,
So what?
Let the children beg,
Living in temporary shacks was no fun,
Many babies died before their lives had barely
begun,
Those that survived grew up to be,
Cheap labour in a factory,
Some lived as street urchins on their wits,
Or descended into the gloom of the pits,
There was always the workhouse to beckon you in,
A hell on earth,
A human dustbin.

George Lansbury The Son

Dutiful the son stood waiting for his dad,
Outside the coalmine,
Where most of the men had worked,
Since they were as young as him,
Nobbut a lad.

Pa had told him about gas explosions,
Pit props collapsing,
The roof falling in,
So the son decided it wasn't the job for him,
He'd worked hard at school,
Though it was only a basic education,
He was at the edge of a new horizon,
Born out of poverty,
He grew up to change the nation,
This boy who whistled as he waited for his dad,
Went into battle carrying the pacifist flag,
Gave his voice to the poor and weak,
Could turn into a ball of fire when he started to
speak,
So take a long, hard look,
At this special son,
Chosen by God,
Before his life had even begun.

CHAPTER TWO

At the age of fourteen George Lansbury returned to the world of work. This time he tried his hand at being a wholesale grocer though it sadly proved unsuccessful. He then got a job as a manager of a coffee bar which unfortunately didn't provide him with long term employment.

In 1875 George Lansbury senior passed away and it must have been a year tinged with sadness, but also joy for George met for the first time a girl called Elizabeth Brine. Bessie, as she was known was fourteen years old and the daughter of Isaac Brine, a local sawmill owner. It was probably the most important moment of his young life for Bessie became his childhood sweetheart and the backbone of his existence.

George had great confidence in his abilities as an organiser so he decided to go into business with one of his brothers. Their choice of working as contractors for the Great Eastern Railway proved to be a big mistake for they hadn't realised the dangerous nature of the occupation and a series of accidents led to its failure.

One striking thing about these misfortunes is just why did a young man who appeared to have a strong work ethic, possessed a more than average intelligence and a tenacious character somehow not be able to turn it to his advantage? As we shall see his miseries were sadly far from over.

There was however, one thing in George's life that was running smoothly and that was romance. Bessie Brine, the girl who had caught his eye in Whitechapel Church consented to becoming his wife and they married in 1880. The minister conducting the wedding ceremony being their friend, the rector of Whitechapel, Mr. J. F. Kitto.

By 1884 the Lansbury family had grown to include three children and due to lack of any decent employment they decided to move to the other side of the world, to Brisbane to be precise. They waved goodbye to 45 Montague Street, Mile End, New Town, Whitechapel and set sail for Australia.

The journey to the land of milk and honey, as it was advertised was not an easy one, Bessie spent most of the trip confined to their cabin. Virtually the whole family suffered from seasickness and the boat almost foundered in a monsoon to add to their wretchedness. Mr. Lansbury however, possessed sea legs and made the best of the journey by disembarking at every port they visited en route. He enjoyed sampling the different cultures and what an education it must have been for him.

Throughout this ordeal one thing kept them going and that was the exciting new life that lay ahead. Seduced by the promise of year round sunshine and plenty of employment, Down Under must have seemed like they were on their way to heaven on earth.

When they finally arrived on foreign soil all their dreams were shattered almost immediately for they had been victims of a cruel deception. The family spent that first night in a hostel for immigrants and they had to face up to the fact that life had taken a definite turn for the worse.

The situation in Australia was dire for there wasn't enough work for the residents, let alone anyone else and it took weeks for George to find any kind of job. The man who had taken the brave step of trying to do the very best thing possible for his little family was reduced to the demeaning rank of a labourer. Stone crushing, which was such a strenuous, back- breaking employment it was used as a deterrent in the workhouse back in dear old Blighty. Mr. Lansbury stuck it out as long as he was physically able until the relentless heat began to take a toll on his health and he managed to find a better position as a van driver transporting meat. It also paid better wages, but this job did not last long because he was given the sack for refusing to work on a Sunday due to his Christian beliefs.

Yet again Lansbury was out searching for work and found a position as a farm labourer. The family packed all their meagre belongings and moved eighty miles inland. It comes as no surprise that this endeavour was also doomed. The farmer had deceived George about the conditions they would have to live in and about the things he was expected to do on the farm. Mr. Lansbury and his family had many months of suffering ahead of them until he was able to get out of the contract. Bessie was forced to cook outside on a campfire and she had not only her own three children to feed, but also another member of the Lansbury clan they had taken with them.

Out of the contract George worked for a brief spell on a parcel delivery van then he did a stint as a groundsman at Brisbane Cricket Club.

After the worst twelve months of their lives the Lansburys returned to the East End, the fare having being paid by Isaac Brine. Mr. Brine took on his son-in-law as a veneer dryer at the sawmill and the family set up home next door to the business at 105, St Stephen's Road, Old Ford.

It was the perversion of the truth that had led to the Lansburys embarking on their Australian disaster. Lied to by the agent before they set off that there was plenty of work on the other side of the world had been the catalyst for their trip. Mr.

Lansbury burned with righteous anger and he was determined to inform as many people as he possibly could the truth about emigration to the colonies. This terrible personal experience added weight to the campaign and began GL's political career.

In 1882 George was appointed to the Poor Law Board that oversaw Poplar Workhouse and his Christian beliefs were soon responsible for sweeping changes. GL thought everyone was equal, be they pauper to King, male or female, regardless of skin colour and denomination. There are many verses in the Bible that mention this and I am going to quote one : -

Galatians C3 V28. There is neither Jew nor Greek, there is neither bond nor free, there is neither male nor female, for ye are all one in Christ Jesus.

The workhouse inhabitants were treated very badly, for poverty was seen as not only a criminal offence, but also the fault of the individual concerned. A place where a family whose breadwinner may have been killed in a mining accident no better thought of than the offspring of an unmarried prostitute. They were a drain on resources and a blight on society, the class system of course very much in evidence.

In Poplar Workhouse conditions were particularly bad, in no small measure due to the Officers in charge. An audit took place which revealed some very interesting facts that fraudulent practices were occurring. The itemised books showed linen and other quality products had been purchased while the stores contained the cheapest materials and food unfit for human consumption. The cash difference instead finding its way into some of the worker's pockets. So the paupers had really suffered at the hands of the people supposed to be caring for them. George Lansbury had many innovative ideas to improve the lives of the poverty stricken and so good were they, quite a number were rolled out across the country.

Having a heart filled with love for others is one thing, having the opportunity and determination to follow through is another. Much of Lansbury's social reforms would never have got off the ground without the most necessary item on the list, cash. It came from ordinary working people, some from GL's wealthy gentry friends, a lot from philanthropists. Mr. Lansbury, luckily had a knack of extracting money from as many sources as he was able for a variant range of causes.

Dear Mr. Lansbury

Dear Mr. Lansbury,
I'm writing you this letter,
With grateful thanks,
For making the East End far better,
You improved so many people's lives,
On hard work, determined, you thrived,
Without glamour and glitz,
You used your wits,
To get by,
As you answered yet another rally cry,
No airs or graces,
Nothing grand,
Some labelled you a firebrand,
When you stood up and said your piece,
It filled opponents with unease,
They didn't want to hear the truth,
Speeches outlining reform, reproof,
Age did not dim your eye,
Still responded to the rally cry,
So I end this little note,
Here's a whole book of words that I devote,
To you Mr. Lansbury, my hero,
A bowler-hatted East End superhero.

Bessie

You put up with so much in your time,
Your shoulders broad,
Your smile kind,
Aged fourteen as Miss Elizabeth Brine,
You met your future spouse to be,
Were impressed by his personality,
He stood out in Whitechapel Church from the rest,
Even at that tender age,
Who knew the place he would take on life's stage,
You both chose well for you'd met your match,
Soul mates able to work through the roughest
patch,
The twists and turns of life knitted you together
neatly,
George was devoted to you completely,
For over fifty-three years you shared married life,
Mr. Lansbury knew he had been blessed to have
you for his wife.

The Poplar Workhouse

Demeaned, degraded, dejected,
The workhouse inhabitants were society's
rejected,
Until Mr. Lansbury was appointed to the Poor Law
Board,
Wondered why they could not afford,
To be given better care,
The staff soon knew that he was there.

Summoned by a bell for breakfast,
A bell for lunch,
A bell to tell you to rise,
A bell to go to bed,
Mr. Lansbury enquired if there was a bell to tell
you
Today you should be dead.

So the new broom swept through the place,
Out went crushing stones as a chore,
The workhouse now had a benign face,
Lansbury changed the rules forevermore.

The pauper enjoyed a better fate,
At last some decent food,
Found its way to every plate,
Instead of mouldy, dried up fare,
The cupboards now were never bare,
No more officers growing fat,
Off the backs of the poor,
"Good old George" saw to that.

CHAPTER THREE

Mr. Lansbury joined the Liberal Party and became ward secretary, then general secretary for Bow and Bromley Radical Association. He was taken on as a campaign agent and was so good at it that all three of the candidates he assisted achieved election success. (Individually, not all three in the same election, then again I don't suppose Lansbury would have in any way been phased by running multiple campaigns.) This led to him being urged to stand for Parliament himself, though George declined the offer because an MP at that time was without financial recompense. Truly, it was done totally gratis which seems amazing in today's political money centric climate.

It wasn't however, just the lack of a wage that put off GL, as he became affectionately known, for his life long Liberal support was dwindling fast. There were two good reasons for this, firstly the Liberals failed to endorse the eight hour working day. Secondly, and perhaps more importantly they were lukewarm in their support of another of Mr. Lansbury's causes which was the Votes for Women Movement.

In 1892 Lansbury resigned from his position and joined the Socialist Democratic Federation (SDF). He put his all into helping them, travelling the length and breadth of Britain in the process, speaking at rallies and supporting employees who had grievances with their bosses.

One thing GL did set aside however, was his Christian faith for the SDF was a Marxist organisation. Mr. Lansbury had been influenced in his decision by the uncaring attitude of local clergymen to the poor inhabitants of their parish. George and Bessie up to then had been stalwart in their service and attendance at Whitechapel Church, but they walked away from God and signed up with the East End Ethical Society. The Lansbury children were sent to the group's Sunday School and for a while life was without spiritual nourishment.

Mr. Lansbury stood for election in 1895 but he only managed to get a small percentage of the vote in Walworth. After much pondering GL gave up his job at the sawmill and took a salaried position as the full time national organiser for the SDF. Circumstances intervened when his friend and father-in-law Isaac Brine passed away suddenly in 1896. Mr. Lansbury accepted that his family duties came before his professional ones and he returned to Bow to take over as manager of the Brine Sawmill and Timber Yard.

In 1901 a new Bishop of Stepney was inaugurated to preside over two hundred parishes containing two million inhabitants. His name was Cosmo Lang and he was no stranger to the East End having helped in its reform twenty years previously while a student at Oxford. Lang eschewed inspecting the area in a chauffeur driven car, instead he used public transport. Surprised and saddened to find so much poverty and deprivation still in evidence Lang soon made the acquaintance of George Lansbury. They both joined forces in the Central London Unemployed Body which was a government organisation to fight unemployment.

Lang worked tirelessly raising much needed funds at Church Conferences to provide more clergymen and lay people in Stepney and Poplar. His meteoric rise first to Archbishop of York and then Archbishop of Canterbury sadly caused Lang to turn away from his radical roots. He was responsible however, for a very important event in the life of GL. It was the encouragement of Cosmo

Lang that caused a shift in the most powerful weapon in Mr. Lansbury's armoury which were his Christian Socialist beliefs.

Eventually with Lang's words beginning to take effect Mr. Lansbury started to find his way back to faith by an occasional attendance at a church in Barkingside. Discovering there was to be a special service at Bow Church, Bow Road, Stepney with a visiting minister George made a decision to speak to the man afterwards. Not wanting to be spotted in the congregation by his neighbours he sat behind a pillar out of sight, but of course he couldn't hide from God. When all George's questions had been answered to his satisfaction he took St Francis of Assisi as his ideal Christian and was, much to his surprise welcomed back into the fold. From then onwards Mr. Lansbury, who could never have been called lukewarm dedicated his life to serving God. He became a member of Bow Church and over the years he was a Sunday School teacher, a youth leader, he served on the Church Council, he was a representative at the Deanery Conference, he ran men's clubs, a branch of the Temperance Society and he served as a churchwarden. GL was also a staunch and very vocal supporter of the church football team. His encouragement inspiring them to win on many occasions when matches were not going in their favour. With his wife Bessie, who also played an active role in the Church they were familiar faces among the congregation for over forty years.

In 1900 Mr. Lansbury stood in what was described as the khaki election and he denounced the Boer War as being wicked. He brought pacifism to life as a modern movement which up to then had been the domain of small groups like the Quakers. The Society of Friends as they are also known have a long history of being anti war, as far back as 1660 in fact. In Mr. Lansbury's hands it looked for a time that his influence had tipped the balance, but it was not to be. To George it was so simple, if we all loved one another then we wouldn't be consumed with the hatred that war breeds between nations.

In 1903 Mr. Lansbury was elected to Poplar Borough Council and he remained there until his death in 1940.

In The Footsteps Of George Lansbury

The spirit of the East End burns just as brightly,
As decades ago when George Lansbury walked
nightly,
Through dark, damp streets back to Bow,
To Bessie and his family,
For he loved them so.

One fault in his critic's eyes,
His Christian faith which could not be contained,
A few memorials are all that remain,
Of "Good old George",
The East End's friend,
Champion of women's rights,
Pacifist to the end.

Weeks spent in prison cells confined,
Yet still he stood strong, not undermined,
The man of steel remained as immovable as ever,
Retire? No way,
He kept up with his endeavour,
To yearn for peace,
To burn from release,
From the shackles of inequality,
Discrimination,
Age did not diminish his conviction,
He endured another stay in prison.

The light may have sadly been extinguished,
But the memories remain,
It's up to us to shout the rally call,
To follow in his footsteps,
For those beliefs,
Stand up just as tall.

The Wishing Well

I stand beside the wishing well,
Silver coins jangling in my hand,
To throw down into the dark abyss,
Listen for the faint splash as they land.

Over my shoulder I carry the flag of pacifism
unfurled,
My wish is simple,
Yet virtually impossible to achieve,
I hope for peace and unity around the world,
If I wish hard enough and believe,
Perhaps it will happen this secret dream of mine,
And war can become a memory from a bygone
time.

A Prayer For Peace And Unity

Standing at the gate I pray,
Let it always be this way,
Hope for another day,
Our Father in Heaven.

Send us your love and grace,
Let it surround this place,
Strength in everything we face,
Our Father in Heaven.

Give us faith in your power,
Let be seen in every shower,
That grows our food and every flower,
Our Father in Heaven.

Forgive us our foolish ways,
Let it be reflected in our praise,
Prayer and thankfulness fill our days,
Our Father in Heaven.

Let us rise up and unite,
As one body to fight the good fight,
For peace let us burn forever bright,
Our Father in Heaven.

CHAPTER FOUR

In 1901 George Lansbury met a man called Joseph Fels and it was a fortuitous event because he soon became one of the most important people in the story of GL

Fels was an extremely wealthy American soap manufacturer with a social conscience. Along with his wife Mary they were vocal in the support that they gave to various causes. Joseph raised the subject of women's suffrage and befriended politicians in the United States and England who he thought would have most impact on getting women the vote. Mary thought women should not behave in a compliant, passive way, but strive by their own efforts to find a place in life. She gave several talks in England on this matter and was quick to invite George Lansbury to go to America and speak at the Woman's Suffrage Council in Philadelphia. Unsurprisingly GL just as quickly accepted. Mrs. Fels was also a supporter of the peace movement which was gaining in popularity at that particular time.

There was one voice of opposition from a surprising quarter however, Bessie Lansbury wrote to Mr. Fels saying how the militant behaviour of the Suffragettes was not something she could accept. Fels sided with GL believing that violence was necessary to achieve their goal.

The Russian Movement was another area where Fels and Lansbury became interlinked. There were many sympathisers, but they were reluctant to back up ideology with hard cash. A meeting was set up between Fels, GL and two devotees of the cause and Joseph agreed it would be a good idea to get rid of some of his surplus money by making them a loan. After a taxi ride to the bank the four men made their way to Brotherhood Church where Lenin was giving a speech. Fels came under the spell of the passionate oratory though he didn't have a clue what was actually being said. Mr. Fels still kept a common sense attitude to his money and the promissory note stipulated when the seventeen hundred pounds interest free loan should be paid back.

Mr. Lansbury had many plans to improve the conditions for the poor people in Poplar, but they were rejected by the Poor Law Board. GL didn't get discouraged but bided his time and managed to get several socialist members including Will Crooks onto the Board. Then GL, all guns blazing began to get his own way.

Back to Joseph Fels the Naptha-Fels soap manufacturer and GL persuaded him to buy Laindon Farm which was standing empty. Twenty miles out of London in Essex, the one hundred acres was leased to Poplar Guardians by Fels for a peppercorn rent. It became home for two hundred paupers from the Poplar area who were first set to work clearing the land, planting orchards and gardens. Even a small river was dammed to create a reservoir.

Mr. Lansbury was not satisfied enough was being done and he didn't rest on his laurels. Laindon was successful, but was on too small a scale to even scratch the surface of the dire need of the destitute East Enders.

Walter Long was the Conservative president of the newly established government body set up to help the unemployed. It was made up of borough councillors, London County Councillors and anyone sympathetic to the subject. Long appointed GL to the committee which arranged to send the unemployed to two farm colonies operated by private charities.

Once again Mr. Lansbury called on the generosity of Joseph Fels and persuaded him to contact Walter Long. Fels offered to buy the 1,300 acres estate of Hollesley Bay Agricultural College and put it at their disposal for three years. Long agreed to the plan and Mr. Lansbury became the full force behind the scheme. During the winter of 1905-06 he spent all his weekends at the farm, setting up classes, lectures and recreational activities for the inhabitants.

Dear Mr. Lansbury We Really Need Your Help

Dear Mr. Lansbury we really need your help,
The country's on its uppers,
The world's in such a mess,
I know how hard you worked to reform the East
End,
Solved crisis after crisis,
You were everybody's friend,
You witnessed deprivation and destitution,
So with the help of Joseph Fels,
Came up with a solution.

Better food in the workhouse,
You instigated so many schemes,
Your ideas became realities,
Not remained as idle dreams.

We could learn so much from your achievements,
Never afraid to display emotion,
You fought so hard against inequality,
To all your causes showed tireless devotion.

Song For George Lansbury

Out of the door you stepped on it,
Gave your all and that's a fact,
For minority causes you didn't hesitate one bit,
Popped on your bowler hat,
And you were away,
Down Bow Road at a pace,
East Enders loved your distinctive face,
You are a local hero that's for sure,
Constant interruptions at your door,
But you'll be remembered forevermore,
In your beloved Bow.

Out of the door you stepped on it,
Gave your all and that's a fact,
Spoke out in Parliament you didn't hesitate one
bit,
Popped on your bowler hat,
And you were away,
Through the streets of Westminster at a pace,
Londoners loved your distinctive face,
You should be a national hero,
That's for sure,
Hundreds of letters through your door,
But you'll be remembered forevermore,
In your beloved Bow.

Out of the door you stepped on it,
Gave your all and that's a fact,
Stood up for peace you didn't hesitate one bit,
Popped on your bowler hat,
And you were away,
Round the world at a pace,
Pacifists loved your distinctive face,
You should be an international hero,
That's for sure,
Mocked and jeered at for trying to prevent war,
But you'll be remembered forevermore,
In your beloved Bow.

George Lansbury's Silent Partner

At every event the silent partner was never far
away,
Sitting quietly waiting,
Never getting in the way,
They were a perfect pair,
This friend he loved to carry,
Indeed you might think it was his wife,
Who shared his life,
Bessie Brine, his childhood sweetheart,
He went on to marry.

But no, his bosom buddy, best mate,
Was sent round after meetings,
Because it held more than a collection plate,
Like Laurel and Hardy he loved his bowler hat,
Hated to be parted from it,
Raised it in greeting,
When he stopped for a chat.

The Battlefield

On this battlefield sword in hand,
We march victorious to the Promised Land,
We stride out,
Spirits high,
We faced death,
But we'll never die.

Our King awaits at Heaven's Gate,
The Light of the world,
Ever shining,
Ever new,
Effulgent elation,
Joyous jubilation,
When we hear the golden trumpet sound,
Filled with faith and hope anew.

CHAPTER FIVE

One of the things that really set George Lansbury apart from most of the other politicians of that era was his whole hearted support for the Suffragette Movement. He wasn't alone in this, but he probably did much more than any other man of his generation to further their cause. Way back in his career long before the Votes for Women Campaign, GL was there with equal rights uppermost in his mind. He stood in the 1909 election as an Independent Socialist candidate in Middlesbrough though he secured only a small number of votes.

It wasn't until 1910 that Mr. Lansbury became an MP. Aged 52 he won the seat for Bow and Bromley in the General Election. In 1912 he resigned his seat to force a by-election and stood as a Suffragette Candidate which didn't however, make him popular even among women and he lost to a Conservative.

In 1913 George addressed a Women's Social and Political Union Rally held at the Albert Hall when he openly defended the violent methods used by the Suffragettes. He told them to use whatever means to achieve their goal. For this George was arrested, charged with incitement, convicted and after an appeal was dismissed, sentenced to three months imprisonment. He immediately went on hunger strike and was released after four days. Although under the so called Cat and Mouse Act he was liable to be arrested at any time GL was left alone.

The East End Federation of Suffragettes began in shop premises in Bow Road before moving to Roman Road. Number 39 Bow Road became the home of the Lansbury family and the double fronted property featuring a Greek style porch was soon open house for political gatherings and folks down on their luck. It must have been very noisy because the Lansburys had eleven children, not forgetting George junior who sadly died as a youngster which meant Bessie had given birth twelve times.

Votes For Women

Votes for women came the cry,
Laughed almost to oblivion,
Mr. Lansbury joined the Pankhurst's on their
crusade,
Tried his best to help their cause,
Fell on his sword,
Resigned his Parliamentary seat,
To stand as a Suffragette Candidate,
But suffered ignominious defeat,
Still he carried on giving his voice,
Believed all women should have a choice,
They didn't sit back quietly on the fence,
Gave a good defence,
Chained themselves to railings,
Emily Davison gave her life,
When she threw herself under the King's horse,
Many labelled them as cranks,
Though we have the Suffragettes to thank,
For putting up such a fight,
To give us ladies an equal right.

In The Front Room 39 Bow Road

George Lansbury sat in his front room,
At 39 Bow Road, desk facing the window,
He could watch the world go by,
Hear the tramcar's clatter,
Housewives' mumbled door step chatter,
From the parlour window,
Warm in summer,
GL kept his benevolent eye on Bow,
Never lost touch with his constituents,
Always in the know,
Frequent callers at the door,
Begging letters by the score,
Threw most of them in the bin with a sigh,
Watched the East End life pass by,
Children on their way to lessons,
Parishioners to confession,
Steam lorries carrying bales of hay,

Barrels to public houses conveyed by horse and
dray,
Heard the clip clop of their shoes,
The heels of clogs,
As they passed his window,
Folks minded their P's and Q's,
Shop workers, factory workers,
All ages shapes and sizes,
Mr. Lansbury sat waiting to solve the latest crisis,
Writing letters to the broadsheets,
Pondering on world events,
His finger on the pulse of life in busy London
streets,
Fortified by frequent cups of tea,
His brain was never idle,
Working tirelessly for the latest cause,
One battle fought,
Another sprang up soon of course,
His efforts earned him no fortune or fame,
History books barely mention his name,
But in Bow, Lansbury's influence will forever shine,
With plaques and flats to celebrate,

A man way ahead of his time.

Read All About It

Busy East End streets filled with voices shouting
out the wares,
From the market stall holders to the newspaper
vendors,
Calling " Read all about it! Read all about it!
Good old George is in the news again,
Everybody round here knows the name,
The kids in the school yard chant the same,
Good old George he's our friend,
No doubt about it,
So come on folks read all about it,
He's spoken out for us in the House again,
I'd like to shake his hand,
Good old George he's not grand,
So come on lady he helped you get the vote,
Buy a paper and read all about it,
Lansbury's given Churchill some stick again."

CHAPTER SIX

George Lansbury possessed many talents and he used them to their full potential. He began his writing career with essays produced by members of Whitechapel Young Men's Association. Many of their efforts were so filled with agnostic articles that the minister started a Bible study class to redress the balance, so ignorant were they of the Gospel.

In later years GL turned his attention to composing many letters to the broadsheets. He became editor of The Daily Herald and used this platform, especially during the First World War to get across his pacifist beliefs. Mr. Lansbury travelled to the Western Front trenches so he could send his eye-witness accounts of the conflict.

In 1925 he turned to a new venture, a publication entitled Lansbury's Labour Weekly which was for a while a rather popular purchase. To boost flagging sales GL stumbled upon some left wing recordings which had been banned by the record companies. Due to the covert nature of the enterprise these records were labelled inside the newspaper office and some mistakes occurred.

Renditions of The Red Flag or The International could be bought, perhaps a talk by Ramsey MacDonald. Even Mr. Lansbury produced one and it was a stirring rally cry. This is a little snippet of what he said : -

"The British Labour and Socialist Movement is in fact a revolutionary movement. We desire to change the present, chaotic, unchristian, immoral, industrial system into one based on cooperation, justice and love. We believe it is as possible to grow food to eat, build houses to live in as it is to make a road, construct a sewer, build a school or generate light as social services. We see no need for mere money making. When we sing The Red Flag we shall sing to the revolutionaries of whom it is said His blood red banner streams afar who follows in its trail. Because our red flag stands for the same oneness of human life embodied in the words he has made of one blood all nations of the earth. For keeping this revolutionary doctrine he was crucified. Many a thousand others have been torn asunder, slain with swords for doing the same. In our days thousands are in prison throughout the world whose sole crime is they believe in true freedom. When we sing The International we proclaim our faith in human brotherhood. When we sing On We March then we the workers and the rumour that you hear is the blended sound of battle and deliverance drawing near. We must resolve that come what may in dark days and bright we will keep our faces toward the Light, confident and sure that the workers of the world will win emancipation, if we have faith in one another, they fight on and thank God."

Mr. Lansbury was the author of numerous books from two volumes of an autobiography to recounting his trip to Russia. Never a wealthy man the royalties came in useful and they make very interesting reading for he conveyed his thoughts very well.

It's Hell Here, No Lie

This is our last foray,
Long overdue we march to a different drumbeat,
Tune overplayed in our heads,
These are the glory days of legend,
But the battle is yet to be won.

How do we stop that ticking?
Time echoing in our ears,
Adrenaline rushes as we launch forth,
Stifling our innermost fears.

Battle weary over the hill we trudge,
Filthy, a half empty parade,
The others buried in fields,
Battered, destroyed before we even began.

What is our motto?
Do or die!
Sit on the bench,
In the trench,
It's Hell here, no lie.

No adventure, those home spun myths,
This is bitter, raw edged,
A soul destroying mess,
Swallowed up in a black pit,
Listen to the cries of distress,
Still we go on,
Less and less,
Everyday.

In this life I've tasted so little,
Mostly harsh reality and pain,
Death beckons with a cold hand,
I wait to be pushed through that gate,
To oblivion or Heaven,
For the bullet that surely bears my name.

Power Over The Poor

The poor were kept in their place,
Ground down,
Doors slammed in their face,
Hidden away out of sight,
In slum filled streets,
Dimly lit at night,
Crime had the upper hand,
The powers that be didn't want to help or
understand,
A low paid workforce with no choice,
No voice to complain,
Stand up for them, intervene,
Make wrongs right again,
Poor people with rags for clothes,
Going to work in winter without any shoes,
To the rich they were the cogs,
Kept the money rolling in,
The Master took better care of his dogs,
Than his employees, shame on him,
Long hours,
Dangerous conditions,
Rotten food,
No wonder the match girls smeared the Gladstone
statue with their blood,
Yet the rally cry was answered,
Things began to change,
With the help of social reformers like George
Lansbury,
To usher in a more civilised age,
Now the maligned worker, women and the poor,
Had a champion full of energy,
Not an ivory tower sitter,
But a doer.

Life In The East End

Life in the East End was dire and grim,
Buoyed up by rhyming slang,
Deep community spirit within,
Streets filled with rows of slums,
Sharing facilities was pretty glum,
Even Mr. Lansbury washed outside with a bucket of
cold water,
But at least they had the protection of bricks and
mortar,
A bed to call their own,
Large families, clothes handed down, outgrown,
No aspirations, low pay,
Dangerous chemicals used in the match factory,
Near Bow Church owned by Bryant and May,
The statue of Gladstone was testament to
deprivation,
After suffering a few more years they set on
reparation,
On strike those lowly match girls,
What a shock,
Fed up with hardship, phossy jaw,
They stood as one like rock,
Getting rich off the backs of the uneducated poor,
No words George Lansbury said were truer,
The poor are that way because they have been
robbed,
No wonder the East Enders loved him so and he
was mobbed,
The man who held his ground with a cheerful
disposition,
Said his piece, got things done,
Improved the human condition.

CHAPTER SEVEN

Mr. Lansbury's greatest triumph was Poplarism. Local authorities had to bear the financial cost for the unemployed so if the area was a poor one it meant a higher rate. GL decided that it was going to be altered and the way to achieve this aim was to levy the payment so that the wealthy London boroughs who had no workhouse to fund could afford to pay more.

The residents of Poplar were instructed by Mr. Lansbury to withhold payment of their rates and rent which led to the councillors being arrested. Sentenced to six weeks in prison the crowd of people who had waited outside the courtroom followed them through the streets to the jail. GL addressed the mass from his cell and for the duration of their incarceration the twenty-five male councillors, among them George's son Edgar Lansbury conducted their business inside. The five female members of Poplar council which included George's daughter-in-law   Minnie Lansbury nee Glassman were taken by cab from Holloway Prison to Brixton Prison to attend meetings.

On a regular basis Mr. Lansbury spoke through prison bars to his supporters. News spread to the neighbouring boroughs and the councillors from Stepney and Bethnal Green chose to withhold their rates too.

In the end George achieved his goal and there were many changes brought about because of the action. The jubilation though was sadly short-lived for Minnie, weakened by the wretched conditions of the jail succumbed to pneumonia. She was only thirty two years old, but a woman way ahead of her time, a Suffragette, a member of the War Pensions Committee and who strived to help the poverty stricken without thinking of the personal cost. For this she was dearly loved by the East Enders who mourned her loss. Her coffin was carried along Bow Road by relays of ex-servicemen, proceeded by five hundred unemployed men and followed by a crowd of mourners which included virtually all the political and municipal leaders of East London. At the cremation service by request of George Lansbury the congregation sang The Red Flag. A beautiful clock was fixed to the side of Electric House as a memorial.

Mr. Lansbury paid tribute to his beloved daughter-in-law with these words: -

"Minnie in her thirty two years crammed double that amount of years work compared to what many of us are able to accomplish. Her glory lies in the fact that with all her gifts and talents, one thought dominated her whole being night and day; How shall we help the poor, the weak, the fallen, weary and heavy laden to help themselves? When a soldier like Minnie passes on, it only means their presence is withdrawn, their life and work remaining as inspiration and a call to close ranks and continue breast forward."

Mr. Lansbury was offered his first Cabinet post by Ramsey MacDonald and it was ideally suited to him. First Commissioner of Works or First Commissioner For Good Works as Mr. Lansbury was quickly entitled, enabled him to make a big difference in the quality of life for the East Enders. GL drew on another talent or his which was raising some of the funding required from the general public. He was responsible for the instigation of many things, some of which brought criticism. His plan to make a children's boating lake in Regent's Park adjacent to the Hanover and York Gates was one such scheme. Residents of the flats in the vicinity didn't want the kiddies of Camden Town and St Pancras in their backyards as it were. The swings and see-saws were installed despite the protests.

GL had football pitches and race tracks laid, the Serpentine was turned into a swimming pool called Lansbury's Lido. Very few people considered the well being of children in those days, they were slave labour in factories, put out to service as maids or farm servants and expendable.

Giving A Voice To An East End Child

If I could go back to that time, that place,
Show my appreciation face to face,
You elevated me out of the dirt and pain,
Made the East End a happy childhood space.

We were the minority, poor and weak,
Desperate for a champion,
A friend who could speak,
With eloquence, fight our corner,
Give us a voice,
Who realised we didn't live in poverty through
choice.

As Minister of Works you started all those
schemes,
To many we were street urchins, but we still had
dreams,
Of playing football,
Real grass beneath our feet,
Instead of the dirt roads in our back street.

You gave us so much,
We'll always be in your debt,
Showed such kindness to others,
Strangers you'd never even met,
A generous father figure,
"London's Fairy Godfather" no less,
Saved many a lad from a life of crime I guess,
So these are
MY words,
MY eulogy,
MY speech,
Let them flow outwards, reach,
To Heaven's Gate where you surely passed
through,
I give thanks to God for lending us you.

Poplarism - In Memory Of Minnie Lansbury 1889-1922

Rates in the London boroughs were unbalanced, unfair,
Many people complained,
But it took a man called George Lansbury,
To really care enough to force a change,
Mount a well organised campaign, engage,
With the Poplar resident,
Who he advised to withhold their rates and rent.

Much loved and well respected by the gathered mass,
Lansbury led a mini revolution,
Against the wealthy upper class,
The Poplar councillors were sent with him to jail,
But this was one cause not allowed to fail,
The authorities could not silence the non-violent activist,
Devoted socialist, determined protagonist,
Through prison bars he addressed the waiting crowd,
Gave encouragement,
Showed he hadn't been cowed,
By the terrible conditions inside,
His steadfast example turned the tide,
Stepney and Bethnal Green followed Poplar's lead,
Eventually the rates were levied,
What a glorious victory indeed.

Success though extracted a bitter price,
George's beloved daughter-in-law, Minnie,
Paid the ultimate sacrifice,
Weakened by the prison stay,
She had no strength left to fight,
Pneumonia extinguished her once brilliant light.

George Lansbury The Fighter

George Lansbury was a man who could put up a
fight,
As he marched into battle,
He stood up for the poverty stricken,
He stood up for equality,
He stood up for human rights.

George Lansbury was a man who had no thought
of self,
He thought about the poverty stricken,
He thought about the bored East End child,
He thought about the workhouse inhabitants
health.

George Lansbury was a man who didn't stay on the
sidelines,
Condone,
He voiced his opinions in the Houses Of
Parliament,
He voiced his opinions in the Albert Hall,
He voiced his opinions in the broadsheets,
He voiced his opinions in the streets,
He voiced his opinions in the East End community,
He voiced his opinions at every opportunity,
He achieved so much for all his causes,
He put the needs of others before his own.

CHAPTER EIGHT

Mr. Lansbury wasn't afraid to display his Christian beliefs in political speeches or in letters to the broadsheets. He wrote to The Times in 1932 calling upon those who counted themselves as Christians and wanted to do God's will to unite together. Harnessing the power of prayer to move mountains of ignorance and misunderstanding about destitution. GL thought that the working class shouldn't have to spend all their energies on earning a living and that time should be available on a Sunday to go to a church or a chapel, at the very least a political meeting. George thought people ought to be able to go to the cinema or public house if they really wanted to, but freedom of choice was always uppermost in his mind.

By 1933 George had succeeded Arthur Henderson as leader of the Labour Party and he used his position when Germany withdrew from the League of Nations to give voice to his long held opinions : -

" I would close every recruiting station, disband the Army and disarm the Air Force. I would abolish the whole dreadful equipment of war and say to the world DO YOUR WORST."

It was while opening a bazaar at Gainsborough in December 1933 that disaster struck. Before he addressed a public meeting George fell and badly fractured his thigh. He felt close to death for a while, but thankfully recovered enough to start writing. His six month stay in Manor House Hospital produced a couple of books, part two of his memoirs and My England. The latter's message was that if the miseries in life were chased down then happiness would be set free. Mr. Lansbury's formula for a utopian socialism was to build the New Jerusalem spreading outwards from the streets of his beloved Bow. GL believed that everyone had the capacity to live a good life helping others. He knew the power of prayer and that it clarified and cleared his mind. It inspired him to work harder, ironed out his problems and made his path straightforward. Prayer made him more effective as a politician and much more able to help others.

George's long stay in hospital gave him a tremendous renewal of his Christian faith. He became more passionate and vital in his efforts with the peace campaign thinking that his life had been spared for that purpose. After a period of convalescence with one of his sons in the country, GL using a stick to aid his mobility returned to public life. At seventy-five years of age just when his critics thought he was spent Mr. Lansbury flew higher and further than ever, metaphorically and physically.

In 1935 George Lansbury offered his resignation, but his colleagues persuaded him to stay. He gave a rousing speech in Parliament on the subject of peace and received a standing ovation. Within minutes George's words were ripped apart by Ernest Bevin. This was enough for Mr. Lansbury he offered his resignation again and was adamant he would not continue as leader.

GL was still an MP for Bow and Bromley alongside many other roles ; chair of the No More War Movement; chair of the War Resister's International; Chairman of the Anglican Pacifist Fellowship and President of the Peace Pledge Union. Under the banner of Embassies of Reconciliation he visited the majority of government heads in Europe including Adolf Hitler and Benito Mussolini. He also made a trip to America to meet President Roosevelt. Mr. Lansbury was not naive about the Nazi threat, but he was prepared to live out Christ's command to turn the other cheek.

I Hear The Roar

I hear the roar of ten thousand shells,
Standing among a sea of white memorials,
Heart pounding,
I feel the earth shake beneath my feet,
Smell the gas,
Listen to the screams,
Vision overcast, blood red.

Vivid as if it was yesterday,
Jostling for position in the trenches,
I slide in the mud,
I have brushed a face,
Realise with a shock it matches,
The sepia photograph, but blood red.

Reaching through the generations,
A cool hand takes mine,
I am aghast with grief,
For a man I know only by name,
Long chiselled on a Moorlands village cenotaph,
My tears fall like the rain, but blood red.

I am back in the quiet place,
Only sound that of my own voice,
But it is a voice that must be heard,
I cry out for peace,
Standing among a sea of white memorials,
Arms aloft, in my silk dress, blood red.

Our Message

Our message at last revealed,
Our dream,
Our hope,
Long concealed,
Arises from our kindred breast,
For our King we wear the Royal Crest.

Our Victor has beaten the darkness,
Restored the world to light,
Defeated death,
Its sting removed,
Redeemed,
The Kingdom is in our sight,
For this glorious army,
It is our right,
To dwell free from grief and pain,
In the Promised Land for all eternity remain.

Sunday Morning

Momentarily he hesitates at the Saxon church
gate,
Hand gnarled, ancient,
Work-worn, weary,
Hobbles up the path,
Stick tapping an irregular beat,
On the moss-edged slabs,
Cool in the shade of the spreading tree,
Casting its shadow over generations of graves,
Slowly negotiates the centuries old steps,
Stone curved by boot and shoe tread,
Opens the heavy oak door,
Kneels down before the altar,
Sends up an evocation of prayer,
Gives thanks to God for another day,
Another chance,
To worship and praise,
Lit by the sun's rays,
Through stained glass,
Begins preparations for celebrating mass.

George Lansbury The Orator

When George Lansbury spoke people listened,
To the great orator,
Be it in Hyde Park or busy London street,
Then as leader of the opposition
from his Parliamentary seat,
His words made so much sense,
Though many in his audience did not agree,
With a man who had risen up from nothing,
First hand experience of hardship and poverty,
While the other MPs were dressed up to the nines,
GL stuck to his baggy trousers and reefer jacket,
A man comfortable in his own skin,
No grand gestures or high living,
For this imposing figure,
With distinctive mutton chop beard,
Mocked for his support for Votes For Women,
He marched with the Suffragettes in time,
Didn't care what the world thought of him,
In his heart he knew it was right,
Not for him to toe the Labour party line.

A man of the old school with good manners,
But a modern thinker, not a dreamer,
He could be a kindly Father Christmas,
As First Commissioner of Works,
Laying race tracks and pitches,
But underneath a flash of steel,
When he stood up for the minorities,
The down and outs, down at heel,
Paupers in Poplar Workhouse,
No need for spin, everything was real,
A standing ovation for his speech on peace,
Dashed to pieces in a moment,
Resigned his seat,
But not the cause,
Now he really went into battle,
Travelled the world,
Signed his name,
He did his very best,
Thought all fighting should cease,

To our eternal shame,
We are still crying out for peace.

George Lansbury Addressing the Labour Party Conference in 1935

"I believe that force has and never will bring permanent peace and goodwill in the world.......God intends us to live peacefully and quietly with one another. If some people do not allow us to do so. I am ready to stand as the early Christians did and say, this is our faith, this is where we stand and if necessary this is where we will die."

George Lansbury Addressing The Emergency Peace Talks In America

"I want to say as definite and as clearly as I can that although politically and socially I'm a Socialist, I base the whole of my case against war and for a change in social and economic conditions on the teachings of Our Lord. As found in his own sayings, not the sayings of theologians, but what He Himself said, and I also base my philosophy of life on the fact that every religious teacher, every philosopher the world has ever known has always taught that the law of life was not domination."

"I'm quite confident if everybody will only face up that we have all sinned and we've all come short, not only of the Glory of God, but of peace on earth and decent conduct one towards another."

CHAPTER NINE

Mr. Lansbury was responsible for so much change throughout his career. One thing makes him stand out from the other social reformers of the day was the fact that he was always accessible to the public. Strangers would run up to him in the street, address him by his first name as though he was their best friend, he was so loved in the East End.

Many people were short of funds at that time for the East End was populated by the destitute and it was to Mr. Lansbury that they turned. He gave money to the majority of those who requested it with no thought regarding its return. He even took out a bank loan for a perfect stranger so he could set up in business. Bessie was dismayed at her husband's generosity so GL was over the moon when the cash was repaid. Mrs. Lansbury however, was still annoyed for there were so many people in their debt and they were barely scraping along themselves. Her words fell on deaf ears for George couldn't bear to refuse genuine need. He gave without thought of his own situation and I wonder how many of us would act in similar fashion? It's easy to be charitable when our own coffers are full, but the Lansburys were not much better off than their neighbours.

For a man with such a high profile he did most of his journeys around London on his own two feet. Arriving at Euston station in the early hours after speaking at yet another meeting the options for GL, who never had much money to spare were few. Even in pouring rain off he would go, but he was sometimes lucky enough to be picked up by black cab drivers who knew him. For a heavy discount they took him home to Bow Road. Many of them gave him a free ride which shows how much gratitude he engendered. Waiting for him was Bessie who firstly dispensed a strong cup of tea. While dawn broke on a Monday morning Mr. Lansbury sat eating his Sunday dinner which had been kept warm over a pan of boiling water. Perhaps there was time for a couple of hours sleep before GL started his job at the timber yard. He kept to this pattern of life for months at a time for he had been blessed with a good constitution. Described as a bear of a man, well above average height with a large frame and a ruddy complexion GL cut a very imposing and unforgettable figure in the streets of London.

First thing in a morning Mr. Lansbury ventured out to the barbers, for the working class didn't shave at home. If the weather was good he kept his carpet slippers on for the errand. The barber kept a shaving mug and brush solely to use on GL who didn't like being favoured, but the man was adamant. Looking after Mr. Lansbury's distinctive mutton chop beard was an honour for him. Even in the shop premises GL was called on for help from his constituents and it was also the place to catch up on the latest news if he had been away travelling.

Then it was but a few minutes before he was home in the front room and working at his desk on the important issues of the day. When his workload became more than he could cope with his daughter Daisy took on the role of secretary.

To See George Lansbury

One day I spent all the world away,
My feet felt different,
As if on air walking,
The roar of a thousand cheers,
Filled my ears,
My senses heightened,
Like patterns in a kaleidoscope,
Coloured crystals ever-changing,
Yet at every turn I still saw you clearly,
Inexplicable,
How could someone who seemed so tangible,
Be so transient,
How quickly you were gone,
From that busy London street,
That thoroughfare,
From all the millions of people,
Who wander there,
Your eyes were the only ones I wanted to look
into,
To say thank you Mr. Lansbury,
And shake your hand.

Saul And His Epiphany

Saul of Tarsus, a Pharisee,
Persecutor, mocker, killer of men,
Walked hand in hand with hatred,
It was his best friend,
To destroy Christianity his aim,
Twisted by evil,
His soul dark and lost,
Set off for Damascus,
He felt no shame,
Met his epiphany,
A blinding light,
A vision of Christ,
Disabled,
Defenceless without his sight,
Led by his companions the rest of the way.

Jesus appeared before Ananias told him what to do,
Afraid for his life he fulfilled the request,
Went to the place where Saul was staying,
Prayed, laid hands on him,
Restored his sight,
Now refined, baptised,
Begged forgiveness for spilling innocent blood,
A changed man,
Renamed Paul he became a powerful force for good.

I Pray For A New World

I pray for a new world,
With abundant strength to face our weaknesses,
Love to shine a light on those who war against us,
Fortitude for the daily struggle.

Let us show kindness and sympathy for those who
suffer frailty and ill health,
Help us to make change happen,
The sword of truth be our only weapon,
Faith be our constant companion.

Give us insight to perceive and shun wickedness,
And may the word of God be our armour as we go
forth in
the battle against evil

Amen.

CHAPTER TEN

In 1940 Mr. Lansbury was nominated for a Nobel Peace Prize, but none were awarded due to the war. By now his health was beginning to fail and he was admitted to Manor House Hospital. His last Christian pacifist statement appeared in a magazine published in April.

" I hold fast to the truth that this world is big enough for all, that we are all brethren, children of one Father."

Mr. Lansbury died on 7th May, 1940 suffering from stomach cancer. The East Enders mourned his passing with one of his constituents paying tribute - " One could not help loving George Lansbury because there was nothing but love in his heart."

The funeral held in Bow Church was packed with statesmen, ambassadors and hundreds of local people. Many of them rough and ready, hard working ordinary men, but they had tears in their eyes as they reminisced about Good old George, some had pawned wedding rings to pay for his election campaign leaflets. The mourning continued in the streets of Bow as the cortege made its way to the crematorium the residents sang The Red Flag. Mr. Lansbury's ashes were scattered at sea as he had requested for although he loved his country he was an internationalist.

What became of 39 Bow Road? Well it was destroyed by a bomb in the Second World War and a block of flats called George Lansbury House was built on the site. A memorial to stone for GL is on the exact spot and a garden created by public subscription.

A trip to Poplar in 2014 led to a deepening interest in Mr. Lansbury's story. Hearing an actor recount how he had played the role of GL as if he had come back in modern times inspired me to do my version. "From Bow Road To Treading The Boards" is a day in the life of George Lansbury and it was the easiest thing I've ever written. I hoped to make GL get up out of his armchair and walk from the page into the room of the reader. I have no idea if I achieved that, but these following poems are from that book.

From The Wings Please Step Forward Mr. George Lansbury

A Socialist anthem from long gone days,
Sounds in my head,
Like the road of ten thousand voices singing out
praise,
Your image,
Once a black and white flat print,
Is now colour before me,
Living,
Breathing,
Brought to life by my pencil and pen,
My words have enthused, infused,
Surpassed my original intention,
Transcended reality,
Opened up the fourth dimension,
From the wings please step forward Mr. George
Lansbury,
Take your rightful place centre stage,
Put a face to that shadowy figure from history,
I've tried hard to record an accurate depiction,
You're not a character of my imagination,
A work of fiction,
But an embodiment of love and light,
And in your footsteps,
I pick up the sword of truth,
My flag unfurled,
March onwards with the fight.

Goodbye Mr. Lansbury

As I wave goodbye to Mr. Lansbury,
I shout my farewell very loud,
To make myself heard,
About the noisy London Euston crowd,
I say thank you to a man who never sought fame
or glory,
I hope I've done justice to your life story,
I hope I've done you proud,
I've followed in your footsteps,
Though I could never match your prolific output,
You were blessed with an iron constitution, robust
health,
Used the power of the media,
But never sought personal wealth,
You could write a tagline, a byline,
A Daily Herald front page headline,
A political speech for Parliament,
Or a Suffragette meeting in the Albert Hall,
Piles of pamphlets,
Campaign leaflets,
You did your best for them all,
Your words made plenty of copy for the
broadsheets,
A familiar face in busy London streets,
So I salute you Mr. Lansbury,
Mr. Editor,
Accomplished author,
Orator.

Looking At Modern Life
From The Prospective Of Mr. Lansbury

As I look out though dimming eyes,
At my beloved East End skies,
I admit to approving of some of the change,
No more back to back rookeries of a bygone age,
With outside conveniences and cold water taps,
Life was grim,
That's a fact.

But we've lost something along the way,
Love for our fellow man has all but flown away,
When I think of all the time I spent,
In silent prayer, head bent,
Hoping for peace and unity,
To live as a Utopian community.

Were my efforts all in vain?
I look around, feel the pain,
In my heart for times gone by,
I shake my head and wonder why,
Where are all the decent role models for our
youth?
Why do people no longer desire to hear the truth?
I stood up for equal rights,
Not anticipating ladies would want to fight,
Go to battle instead of showing a pacifist face,
Everything seems so out of place.

I can't believe the fact,
Professing faith holds you back,
I yearned that all religions would have one aim,
To end warfare,
I hang my head in shame,
I was held in high regard,
Children chanted my name in the school yard,
I was "Good old George" to folk I'd never even
met,
How easily they forget,
The deprivation, dirt and despair,
Rows of slum dwellings,

Foggy grey air.

I sometimes faced defeat,
But I never gave up,
Or beat the retreat,
Just regrouped,
Drew up new battle lines,
I was way ahead of the times.

So I shout once more the rally cry,
Fellow soldiers it's do or die,
Let's march to the Christian Socialist beat,
You'll suffer hunger, bleeding feet,
But allow your beacon to shine forever bright,
Be an example,
A guiding light,
Let's stride out with confidence anew,
Adjust our sights to what's good and true,
Push ourselves to the limit,
Every chance,
Every minute,
Wave our red banners,
Opposing wrong is our right,
Prepare to be shot down in the fight.

A Sympathy Letter Written By George Lansbury To His Election Campaign Agent

Mr. Blacketer had actually lost his father-in-law, but he treated him like a father.

My dear Blacketer,

I feel I must send you this note. The news of your father's death and burial came as a shock, one which has left me feeling rather sad.

Yet there is no room for darkness for me or you because his life's journey is over and now comes peace. Death is a final mystery because we believe though the body passes our souls remain and these are in the hands of God from whom all Spirit comes.

You travelled a long journey with your father and will feel his loss deeply, but you will I am sure remember loss or sadness only for a night and then comes the dawn and you will have the wholly blessed memory of all you were to each other and also the equally blessed knowledge that though absent in body he is still nearby in spirit.

God bless you both and keep you till the Day dawns and the night of Sin and Death passes away for ever.

Always,

George Lansbury

SECTION TWO
POETRY ANTHOLOGY

Our Story
Mocked And Scorned
My Heart Sings
Faith
Lofty Heights
It's Christmas
Christmas Joy
On This Battlefield
Champion Of Refugees
Let's All Knit Together Into A Beautiful Garment
Operation Christmas Child
To The War Criminal
In My Dream
Homeless
My Only Weapon
Lost Images
Poplar
Petunia
Perdita
We're Under Attack
The Old Man
I Am The Hands
Somebody's Grandmother
Dementia
Fractured By Time And Distance
Heaven
Brave To The End
Amos The Farmer
Walking With Charlie
I Am
One Single Heartbeat
Loneliness Is Like An Iceberg
I Lie Here In My Lonely Bed Now
In The Next Room? Oh Really?
Only Paint
Why Did You Leave With Her?
I Go Down For The Last Time
Our Day Is Over
Autumn
Drifting
The Doleful Melody Of Winter
The Sweet Song Of Springtime

In Praise Of Summer
Divided By Time
I Go Back
Walking With Seth
How Vast
I Stand At The Window
Shadows Of The Past
Love's Old Song
Limited
Top Of The Morning To You
From Church Pew
Glass And Silk
A Raspberry Ripple Sky
The Dream
Christmas A Century Apart
My Jubilant Return
Lamplight
We Stand Here Together

Our Story

This is our story,
But are we going to glory?
Feet weary,
Bodies ready to collapse,
Still we trudge on,
Being spat at, vilified,
Through the busy streets,
Filled with scavenging animals,
Dust getting in our eyes,
Intense heat, sun casting a haze,
Under attack from the flies,
We are on a path of destruction,
Carrying a wooden cross,
Our last hours on earth,
We are to be displayed, grotesque,
For all Jerusalem to see,
As an example to keep the rest in line,
To be jeered at,
Sneered at
With this guy who they call a King,
Travel the pathway of death together.

But why is he being punished?
What charge the crime?
I'm sure he doesn't deserve this fate,
To be on the receiving end of so much hate,
I believe that he speaks the truth,
So I'm going to repent,
There's still time.

Mocked And Scorned

The King surveys His Realm,
A vast expanse under its own rule,
Governed by worldly matters,
Cold, unloving, cruel.

What is this crown?
It's woven out of thorns,
To adorn his brow,
Mocked,
Scorned,
Tortured,
Sentenced,
Put to death,
For speaking the truth,

In free fall,
Spiraling out of control,
His mind set on an achievable goal,
Out of the black swirls,
A sudden flash of light,
A dawn of new reasoning,
A season of flight,
Up to the plate he stepped,
Heart beating loud,
Centre stage,
Shaking,
His nerves on display,
In front of a jeering, sneering crowd,
Quietly left this world,
Slipped away.

The Disciples

Our King is lost,
Our minds are astray,
We are in the depths of despair,
His arms were aloft,
Now misery is our companion.

For He has been taken prisoner,
The war is over,
Battle weary,
Hungry,
Bloodied,
No defence for His crime,
A figure of amusement,
Liable to be tortured at any time.

Our minds set on survival,
Denial,
Keep our heads down,
Stay out of sight,
Before our Leader pays the ultimate price,
For you and me the Saviour's sacrifice.

Now his arms are outstretched,
Head to the sun,
Cries out a forsaken plea,
Bleeding,
Disjointed,
Disfigured,
On the Cross,
Dying for you and me.

We are forgiven,
Redeemed,
If we renounce,
Repent,
Believe.

My Heart Sings

By cool, calm water I sit and dream,
My fingers icy,
Dangling in the stream,
Why I wonder, ponder longer,
Are you out there in blue yonder?
Floating near above the clouds,
That flicker fast above my eyes,
Does it matter that the shadows shroud,
A part of me, the heart of me,
My soul leaps for joy when I think about eternity,
No pain, no war, eternal bliss,
Who wouldn't yearn for this?
Instead of the end, my friend,
No matter how many times I try,
To tell you,
You just laugh and defy,
The thing that makes me unique,
You refuse and do not seek,
Say you desire an eternal flame,
I know many people who crave the same,
So as I lie here in soft grass,
All the black clouds of life soon pass,
With quietness and prayer,
Spirituality, my soul laid bare,
Dwell on this you doubters,
Mockers filled with scorn,
Nothing beats the feeling of a clean slate,
Forgiveness, being reborn.

Faith

If you ask me would I take a journey?
A leap of faith into the unknown,
Uncharted waterways,
Would I make it on my own?
When there is no map reference,
For the piled up problems in my life,
And Google can't solve them this time,
A lot of people sail along without ripples or waves,
And others get nothing but applause,
Even though they misbehave,
I just go on my way,
Treating every one the same,
Realising that the route is tough,
It's no use looking for something to blame,
That's when faith jumps up,
Grabs my hand,
Steers me back on course,
The lighthouse tries its best,
To shine through the mist,
My boat is travelling faster,
As I grow older and closer to shore.

Lofty Heights

Lofty heights aspired to,
Inspired by you,
The best,
I see the road is narrowing,
Our lives near the end, but blessed,
These busy streets,
Well worn by all those feet,
Who worshipped in this Holy place,
Now just as easily erased,
By hatred,
War,
Begin,
End,
Begin again,
The circle turns,
Spinning,
Out of control,
Orbiting,
Spiraling,
It's trailing orange flame,
An apparition,
A vision,
Of hope.

It's Christmas

Triumphant praise,
Let's show our delight,
Rejoice in preparation of this Holy night,
Stars in the heavens shine,
Protective hands from above,
Please keep us all safe in a shield of love.

Season of hope send out across the earth,
Jubilation,
Ring out the bells,
This is a celebration of our King's birth.

Christmas Joy

The bells ring out for it's Christmas time,
Glittering, sparkling, imitation snow time,
Across the nation,
A frantic whirl of festive preparation,
But beneath the glitz,
Often stressful family drama,
Food piled high in living room and parlour,
Almost forgotten, by many cast aside,
The real Christmas Story,
Imparted by the Archangel Gabriel,
A vision of shining glory.

Sing out you carollers loud with praises,
Ring out the bells in Holy places,
From village churches decked with hedge-gathered
holly,
Where the kindly vicar greets you warmly,
Commiserates at yet another wind turned inside
out brolly,
To lofty cathedral where no one knows your name,
Where ever we attend the message is the same,
Verses from the Four Gospels,
Delivered by a well practised lay reader,
Candles burning brightly,
Gold cloth upon the altar.

Rejoice at this birth with all creation,
For a King entered this world without a Royal
Proclamation,
We form one body below the sacred steeple,
One voice, a community of God's people,
At this midnight mass in December,
We look back with wonder and remember,
That silent night when Christ became man,
Prophetic word realised,
Fulfilled God's plan.

On This Battlefield

My travels nearly at an end,
Story almost complete,
But this is one glorious day,
One day when the world falls at my feet,
These feet tired and weary,
But weary I'll stand to the end,
On this battlefield,
I will not yield,
Bloodied,
Broken,
Incomplete,
Deliver me at journey's end.

Champion Of Refugees

He looks down the line,
At the never ending queue,
The champion of wrongs,
Sees they are tired, hungry and blue,
Thousands stand before him,
It's his Christian duty to help them out,
Refugees, their clothes dirty and torn,
Grey faced, malnourished,
On the edge of despair, forlorn,
Even cold water is a luxury,
A simple, cheap bar of soap,
A few kind words,
Gives them cheer and hope,
For a brighter future,
A safe place to stay.

Let's All Knit Together Into A Beautiful Garment

From this lonely platform,
I survey the frightened, weary crowd,
I welcome them with open arms,
Shout my greetings clear and loud.

I'm their self appointed advocate,
To assist in their distress,
On their behalf use the power of my words,
To cry out from the wilderness.

I say to you world leaders,
Some of you should hang your heads in shame,
Because these people are our friends and equals,
Even though we don't yet know their names.

Let's open up the borders,
Allow refugees their basic human rights,
But you deny their suffering,
Don't feel pity at their plight.

To all you European politicians,
Please show acceptance and love,
Embrace the changing pattern of society,
Until the return of the olive branch carrying dove.

Operation Christmas Child

I have my shoeboxes,
Wrapping paper,
Sticky tape,
To pack a gift for a child,
Who has never had much in life,
No big parcels under a Christmas tree,
So with love I fill this box,
Hope the contents delight,
A bar of soap,
Toothbrush and toothpaste,
Then crayons, pencils and a colouring book,
A doll or teddy to cuddle,
And spin an endless story round,
Skipping rope, jigsaw, a bouncy tennis ball,
A facecloth and a comb,
And a card to say you're a special child.

To The War Criminal

In an appearance of mean and tender years,
The flying by of bullets,
Tears enough to drown in,
Exploding shells, overhead,
The sound of church bells,
Whirling in my head wailing sirens,
Screams of the victims,
They live on in my dreams,
What is justice for such evil?
How can you pay?
When you believe what you did was right,
Come what may,
Where is your conscience?
No humanity at all,
While the world sheds a tear,
You say we are deluded the millions who grieve,
All of us actors cast in a part,
The gas chambers just make believe,
The images bear testament,
But still you deny,
Make any excuse,
Lie.

In My Dream

As I sit at the exit,
All the rejected shuffle by,
Eyes downcast, faces grey,
No hope now,
Eternal dismay.

So while there's still chance,
Throw away all your doubts,
Pick up your sword,
Go out to war,
See the battle lines drawn up,
It's you they're waiting for.

Take up your shield,
Defy all the bad,
The armour of truth,
is the right one to have.

Problems discarded,
Bad habits changed,
With God on our side,
We have our defence,
So stay steadfast,
Strong to the end.

Homeless

I sit begging in need of a handout,
Down on my luck,
Lost my job,
On a zero hour contract,
I try my best to keep clean,
I slipped through the cracks in the system,
A crevice opened up,
Swallowed me whole,
All those dreams and aspirations,
I had as a lad in school,
I worked hard,
Now I'm frightened of slipping into the black
morass,
Around me drugs and abuse,
All I want is a bed,
No fancy furniture,
As I sit in the gloom,
Unshaven,
My body cold,
You rush past without a second glance,
Not willing to give me a second chance.

My Only Weapon
Through The Eyes Of A War Photographer

Click, whirr, click, whirr,
I shoot, not a bullet,
But war in front of my camera lens,
My only weapon,
As I run, half bent in camouflage clothing,
Trying to capture yet another battle,
Transmitted round the world,
Full resolution in a moment,
This is war of the modern day,
People follow me on Facebook and Twitter,
But I find no pleasure,
Being popular on social media.

Click, whirr, click, whirr,
As I shoot without a dress rehearsal,
Death in front of my camera lens,
Civilians cast as extras against their will,
No stunt double to take the blast,
Real blood, not imitation,
The audience watching on plasma screens,
Think they know what death is like,
But I cannot convey the smell of fear,
On the old couple who have walked barefoot,
For ten days to find a safe camp.

Click, whirr, click, whirr,
I shoot footage of children playing,
Life in front of my camera lens,
Among the rubble and destruction,
Unable to communicate with words,
I share out the contents of my bag,
Show them film of my family,
Their laughter and joyous faces,
At the antics of my daughter's kitten,
Are the only images I want to remember.

Lost Images Of The First World War

Studio photographers could barely keep pace,
With all those men off to war,
Who wanted to leave loved ones,
An image of their face,
Excited boys who lied about their age,
Sad eyes of fathers posing with worried wives,
And sailor suited toddler sons,
To stand for decades on mantle pieces, pianos,
Hang on walls,
In long-forgotten spinster's halls,
Frames well-worn around the side,
Where trembling hands, held,
Remembered, cried,
Just cold glass to kiss,
The last words on dying lips,
Names of fiancées, husbands, brothers, sons,
Treasured momentoes,
Ephemera,
With uncaring hands slung into skips,
That in a former life were tanks and guns.

Poplar

Poplar has emerged from the neglect of years,
Regenerated, rejuvenated,
With new buildings, restructured,
To inject into its population,
A sense of purpose, hope,
A dream of greater things,
Spotlight, a centre for young folk,
With a studio, film theatre,
Modern technology to help them achieve,
Look to the future,
A fresh start and believe,
In themselves as being equally good,
Following in the footsteps of George Lansbury,
The East End spirit pulsates with a vigorous beat,
In revitalised Poplar,
Fired-up to compete.

Petunia

Petunia the little darling,
Pink and chubby baby face,
Sits giggling, arms waving,
In the garden,
Her favourite place.

Blonde tousled curls,
A dimpled pout,
But her bad moods don't last long,
Brilliant sunshine is soon back out.

Perdita

Oh Perdita you fill the whole world with your
laughter,
Your welcoming smile behind the shop counter,
Makes Pigmania a thriving business for sure.

The till hardly ever stops singing,
Door bell keeps ringing,
As pig pencils and stencils,
Oven gloves and mitts,
Fly off the shelves,
Served with a heavy dose of your wit.

Perhaps a piggy soft toy,
For your little girl or boy,
Teacloths and facecloths,
Pig jigsaws,
Big hugs and discounts,
For regular customers,
If you can't find your heart's desire,
Or of shopping you tire,
Take your time,
Browsing online.

We're Under Attack

Crack, crack we're under attack,
We march in step,
Left, right,
Left, right,
Do or die,
Our mothers cry,
But we keep marching in step,
In line.

The date,
The place,
The war,
Sometimes we don't remember what we're fighting for,
Just pick up our weapons and off we go,
We are as one,
Can't say no.

Crack, crack we're under attack,
Just keep marching,
No looking back,
Don't stop,
We're going over the top,
To victory or defeat,
We listen for the scream of the bagpipes,
All I hear is the rhythm of marching feet.

This is not our battle song,
As we stumble to a slow defeated drumbeat,
Sink into the muddy, blood soaked landscape,
Too late I hear the sound of retreat,
Carried on the faint breeze,
I see a blackbird,
It's head on one side,
In the safety of the trees,
Beak open, warbling a melody,
A lament,
The mournful notes of death.

The Old Man

The old man whispers the words,
He is back on the battlefield,
Scared, his hands shake,
I try to reassure him,
Only a lullaby soothes him,
Some fleeting memories of childhood,
Before the horrors of war,
I am the nurse who tends these frail, old soldiers,
As they live out their last days,
In hell.

I Am The Hands

I am the hands that signed the letter of
conscription,
I am the hands that held the gun,
I am the hands,
The eyes of the enemy,
I am the hands,
The eyes of the child who thinks war is fun.

Somebody's Grandmother

Images of marching men haunt her dreams,
Air raid sirens frantic screams,
He watches his grandmother's mind disintegrate,
Past unravelling
to become this shell,
A pitiful state,
She has gone back to black out,
Rationing her food,
Some days she is afraid to leave her bed,
As the illness sucks all the past,
to the front of her head.

Dementia

Oh silky grey moth that flutters across
the night sky. Grief
beats your wings on a slow distant song
of the moon. As the embers fall, a red hot,
guarded tongue of flame. Burnished bright
by Bull, Blanco and Brasso. A granite
base that was ours. The last bit of
properly, a tombstone. Piercing the
sky, cylindrical. Epitome of Victorian
extravagance, of creativity. Of
craftsmanship, chiselled out of a cloud
of ...Poison I sip as I sit here dull-headed. By
a stream, as the water flows. Giddy. By
locks and houses. Fly by. Carbon copies
of boyhood days. And the mood sombre as
toys flung into skips. Of daydreams, night
scenes. Terror. Glass splintered, fragmented
memories of a grey fantasy. A hollow eyed
man. Sits, crying
about the past, comrades dead
on an unploughed field. What was once
a shroud of white lies. I clap my hands
to the four winds, to the blazing sun. The
valley, the heights. Kneel down. Bareheaded,
I toiled, care worn my hands. Gnarled
ancient as the old wooden gate. I ponder, clouds
reflected in the age old beauty of butterflies
Fritillaries, Cabbage Whites, Red Admirals
salute the Buddleia. Turn and fade away. As I
sigh, furrowed brow. Lined up
in rows we marched as one. Flashbacks
disjointed, catapult me back
in time. The roar of thunder,
under attack. In my uniform, polished.
Gleaming. To absorb the mud
and blood of a vanquished army. A
destroyed artillery. Collapse. Fade out,
to black.

Fractured By Time And Distance

Segmented kaleidoscopic tumbling, I am falling,
Through air, sea below me,
Fractured by time and distance,
No respite,
Spiraling, I feel weightless,
Quivering I shake free of the tendril's grip,
Feel the rip and pain of an open wound
Festering, infected, I slip again,
Below the surface I try to cling on go the debris,
The flotsam and jetsom of life passing by,
But I am suffering from the shakes,
And they slip through my fingers,
As I fall yet again,
Through the time zone, eternity,
My brain is like ice one minute,
Fevered the next,
Music screams in my ears,
In my brain I see printed text,
In this vortex,

The eye of the hurricane,
Hungry and thirsty, but too tired to eat,
My legs are so heavy now,
I'm dragging my feet,
I see dark shapes and shadows,
They reach out to touch me
Laughing and jeering,
But I can't make out their faces,
I can't hear their words,
My eyes are blind now
My tongue furred,
Is this the end?
The final frontier,
I can hear my own heart beat,
So it must be real.

Heaven

Where is the door to push ajar?
To peer round for a fleeting moment,
If we knew just how near or far,
Would death be feared as much?

Are you close by or in another vista?
Can you see loved ones left behind?
Hear how much we've missed you?
Is Heaven's Gate a pearly white?
Or does it blaze eternal in golden light?

Is the path well trodden by all those feet?
Worn down or does it self repair?
Is there ever a long queue?
Do you have to stand in line or rest in an armchair?

Do we ever tire?
Are belongings shared or just ours?
Are there rainbows after showers?
Or does the sun always shine?

Are there streams filled with sweet water?
Do grapes grow on a vine?
Do we have to make our own food?
Bottle our own wine?

Is our glass ever empty?
Are there mountains covered in cloud?
Are there really choirs of angels?
Do they sing really loud?

Are the tapestries of life no longer needed?
In death do we struggle to find our voice?
Do we age and grow weary?
Or stay at the same life stage?

Does a baby stay a baby?
Does an old man lose his stoop?
Do bones hold us together?
Do we still need to go to sleep?

Brave To The End

Brave to the end I lie,

Broken, past mending think I,

Out on these blood soaked fields I will die,

I'm no hero I cry,

All I ask is why?

Turn my face to the sun and sigh,

When my soul leaves my body will it fly?

Upwards through the gunpowder filled sky,

Will I look down on my body from on high?

The stretcher bearers are here, perhaps it isn't goodbye.

Amos The Farmer

Chain link after chain link,
Paperwork to sign, but ink
spills over me,
I take handfuls of pills,
Yet the pain still comes in violent waves over me,
The doctor whispers that it's all over for me.

I look through my bedroom window,
Notice peeling, black gloss paint,
Listen to a mocking blackbird's calls,
Smile at wedding anniversary ornaments, quaint,
I look out at granite hillsides,
At Yorkshire dry stone walls,
Think of discarded muddy wellingtons,
My new winter coat hanging in the hall.

I look out at heather covered mountains,
At weather beaten old shepherd's faces,
Memories of hard graft taming wild, open spaces.

I want time to spend tumbling
while I count each blade of grass,
Instead of waving at rumbling steam trains
through this square of glass,
My window on the world
frames my wildflower meadowland glory,
As I lie here mulling over decades of life,
I pray to God for more pages in my story,
Row upon row of neat runner beans,
Sweet peas that filled childhood jam jars with
fanciful dreams.

Now they all gather to watch me take my leave of
life,
My lad, his children, my ever patient wife,
But my days are not over,
My deathbed recedes,
I'm made of Yorkshire grit, stern stuff,
I've animals to feed,
Hedges to layer,

Hay to stack,
Seeds of harvest to reap,
At the top of my list?
Dip a whole flock of sheep.

So let me out of this vice while I'm still in the
valley,
The shadow of mortality like ice in my veins,
Mr. Garside our village undertaker waits for my
mortal remains,
But he'll have to wait longer,
Because I'm getting stronger,
Until my last gasp I'm still holding the reins,
I'm trying hard to break free of these crippling
chains.

Walking With Charlie

By the water's edge I stand,
A small, smooth pebble in my hand,
Never too old to skim a stone,
Mind wandering,
Time my own,
Charlie at my heels,
Hot breath, excited barks,
I've brought his squeaky toy,
He runs, zig-zagging across damp sand with joy,
Sun behind clouds hidden away,
This stretch of beach is ours today.

I Am......

I am the bullied child who sits all alone,
In tears at vile words on my smartphone.

I am the woman who sits broken and bruised,
By my partner I'm being abused.

I am the man who sits on the streets all alone,
Begging for food, I have no home.

I am the person who sits in the shadows all alone,
I see everything, but I'm unknown.

Do you realise but for fate and pure chance?
It could be you doing the solitary dance.

Who am I?

I am the voice of reason,
I am the honest opinion,
I am the Poet,
I am the control.

One Single Heartbeat

One single heartbeat again and again,
Echoes in my ears,
Hammers in my brain,
One single bed in a one bedroom flat,
One single duvet, one single place mat,
One set of cutlery forlorn in the drawer,
One toothbrush in the bathroom,
No lock on the door,
One single serving microwave ready meal,
Does one single person know how I feel?
One solitary mug sits in the sink,
Waiting for the wine glass from my lonely drink,
One dinner plate I bought from the end of line range,
It was only fifty pence,
But the pattern's a bit strange,
It's really a second,
Like me it's flawed,
Both of us unwanted, rejected, ignored.

Loneliness Is Like An Iceberg

Loneliness is like an iceberg,
We are conscious of its surface,
But it goes deeper than you can see,
Deep into the heart of the lonely person,
Spreads out like a disease through the community.

We become more wary of our neighbours,
Our work colleagues we shun,
Afraid to answer the front door,
Afraid to look at the sun.

Sunlight becomes our enemy,
We close the curtains in every room,
Get into bed,
Pull the duvet over our head,
Live in another region,
Our solitary vacuum.

Interaction is no longer on the agenda,
If we venture out it's with our heads down,
We can no longer make eye contact,
As in our misery we drown.

We look out of city windows,
On bright lights below,
See shadows of people on glass,
Count the folks we'll never know.

No more friendly conversation,
No more social interaction,
No more small talk,
Just a gradual disintegration,
A black hole of despair,
A free fall into depression,
As ice fills my heart and clings to my hair.

I Lie Here In My Lonely Bed Now

I lie here in my lonely bed now,
Nothing but idle thoughts drift through my head
now,
Of happy days in the past,
When I acted out the part in which I was cast,
But all those glorious days are gone now,
Instead a fuzzy haze,
I am in the slough of despond now.

I let my mind flow freely now,
Let the memories unwind,
But they're eerie now,
As a child I could run so fast,
Now the race is over,
I'm clearly last,
I have to use a frame to walk now,
My neighbours call me
"That miserable old cow" now.

People think I'm oblivious to their cruel words
now,
As if it's only my body,
Not my mind here now,
In this unwanted role I've been typecast,
But I try my best not to be downcast,
When the carers talk above my head now,
And I'm referred to in the third person now.

I have no strength left to fight now,
Never more lonely,
No one to hold my hand now,
Friends, husbands, lovers long gone,
No family, I am the only one,
I drift between life and death now,
Dread the curtains being closed,
Around my lonely bed now.

In The Next Room? Oh Really?

In the next room?
I want to take every copy of that poem,
Rip it into shreds and cast it to the four winds,
Everybody wants to cotton wool death,
Package it in a neat box and forget.

I am frantic, searching through your things,
Trying to find your written words,
And anything that holds the unique smell of you,
I want to seal it inside a bottle,
Your essence, before it disappears.

I rearrange the living room furniture,
Take your favourite suit out of the wardrobe,
Place it on your armchair,
So that when I stand in the hallway,
I can pretend you're still there,
Asleep by the fire again.

Only Paint

I mix my paint carefully,
A palette of perfection,
While you sit silently waiting,
Until I decide the angle,
Expression I want to capture,
No hands in view,
They're too complex,
Take the viewer's eye from the face,
And it's that face I want to replicate,
To absorb the medium's embrace.

Just pigment and powder I use to convey,
Intricate lines beneath those eyes of vivid blue,
That twinkle one moment so warmly,
Then quickly change to a icy hue.

It's hard to portray someone you love,
Much easier a perfect stranger,
Who doesn't make your heart beat faster,
And who impressing is of no matter.

Why Did You Leave With Her?

I walk along the water's edge,
As the tide trickles round my feet,
Cool, moist sand between my toes,
I stone skim and dwell on yesterday,
Before I felt overwhelming, drowning sorrow,
Death's clammy, vice like grip,
Stole you away with one hand,
Used the other to rip,
Tear out my heart.

Why did you leave with her?
The harlot,
Unfaithful to me, I'm betrayed,
Was her lipstick a more vivid shade than mine?
Her hips more sinuous?
Her lips must have been more kissable,
You must have been intoxicated on her sparkling
wine.

While I slept on unaware,
You danced to her tantalising tune,
Did she tell you she loved you?
Beneath a waxen moon,
She lied.

As I stirred awake,
You both escaped down into the valley,
Far away now,
I called out your name,
Tried hard to see your shadow,
But guilty, your face was turned away from me.

Your hair was soft in Sunday's twilight,
When we stood below our honeysuckle archway,
I drank deeply from your unique smell,
A mixture of leather, shampoo and soap,
I thought I had you forever,
I would not have slept if I'd known,
That dawn would bring me to this black tomb.

As the birds sing their sweet melody of Springtime,
There is a winter snow storm inside,
My heart frozen in ice.

I look at the book part read,
Log basket waiting to be filled,
A pile of ironing,
Your keys and spectacle case,
All about me nothing but empty space,
I realise I'm crying.

I feel as though I've failed you,
I should have been able to breathe new life into
you,
My kiss rekindle the fire,
But you lie as cold as the marble hearth,
In her bed instead of mine,
Wearing your best suit,
Your face set in an eternal innocent smile.

I Go Down For The Last Time

I stand idly waiting,
Does it matter?
If it's ten minutes or an hour?
Should I linger in case a rainbow appears,
After this heavy sun shower.

Do I care if my final stare?
My unrepentant gaze,
Sees the droplets in a multi coloured hue,
No more lies,
Everything is clear now, true.

Why have I sat so many times on the edge?
Of a high rise flat's window ledge,
Legs dangling and lost my nerve,
After all what purpose do I serve?

Since that day when my bare feet felt cold, damp
grass,
Was it really last spring we held your funeral
mass?
I ran sobbing from your grave,
In death I've been your constant slave.

Waiting for your sign that never came,
Instead this emptiness, every day the same,
Will the manner of my passing cause even a ripple?
No, for in bereavement my family proved fickle.

Tired of my grief stricken face,
Advised me to get another man to fill your space,
Their callous words no comfort in my despair,
Pushed me into another zone beyond care.

No longer fully in this life, I'm at the end,
I walk hand in hand with the final friend,
We listen to the gulls crying overhead,
They'll be my only mourners when I lay cold and
dead.

Our Day Is Over

A day is but an ink blot on the page of the life
book,
A spot on plain white,
Is it untidy scribble?
Or neat copperplate?
Does the spine creak with age?
Voluminous pages,
Or a dull, meagre read of wasted years?
Untasted joys,
No light verses,
But filled with dirges.

Verdigris creeps along the gate,
That once shone lacquered black,
With a painted gold finial,
A house that once brimmed over with laughter,
Stands empty,
Hollow as the soul it crushed,
Plaster has begun to drop from the Victorian walls,
Bricks losing crumbling mortar,
No longer the glue that holds us all together,
As we say goodbye for the last time.

Autumn

Silky, silent tread,
I survey the scene below,
Ancient,
Powerful,
An overwhelming, seething density,
Of an autumnal mist.

Clearing a passage through half empty trees,
A fierce wind doing its best to destroy,
Glorious displays of leaves,
A carpet of fiery hue,
Then a rusty spiral
Of gathered foliage,
Airborne above the forest floor,
Sycamore keys and acorns,
Ferried to fertile ground,
Hopes for saplings,
Fresh growth,
Renewal,
Cycle ever-changing,
Sounds, colours,
Unique smells of the seasons,
All pervading,
Optimistic,
That spring will soon be in the air.

Drifting

Drifting daintily by on slipstreams,
Moonbeams and daydreams,
Vast expanses of empty air,
On fluffy cumulonimbus without a care,
In death weightless and free,
Beneath a sylvan blue sky,
No limit to distance and space,
Leaving no trace,
Unseen as I go floating by.

The Doleful Melody Of Winter

Wind whistles it's doleful melody,
As nature dances to the tune of Winter,
I watch the first fragile fragments,
Reminiscent of a freshly shaken snow globe,
Turn into an all consuming pillow fight,
Of feathery snowflakes,
Transforming the once verdant valley.

Brittle icicles hang from branches,
Decoration for leafless bare boned skeletal trees,
A hopeless sun flickers behind dirty grey clouds,
Attempts to warm the atmosphere,
Gives up, fades away.

Eventually the blizzard clears,
All those tiny ice crystals, stylish, unique,
Have fallen into place,
Become an interlocked jigsaw,
A white carpet-covered landscape.

All is eerily silent, calm,
In the graveyard called Winter,
As nature sleeps,
Dreaming about the birth of Spring.

The Sweet Song Of Springtime

Groups of small white flowers stand bent headed,
Snowdrop sentries heralding the birth of Spring,
I watch the migrating birds returning,
Young lambs in fields happily gamboling,
Unaware of the joy such sights bring.

Listen!
Can you hear the sweet song of Springtime?
Melody carried on the faint breeze,
Intermingled with the blackbird's chatter,
Behold the rainbow's colours,
Viewed through an April shower.

I wander through woods bluebell-carpeted,
My dog, nose down excitedly foraging,
Truffle hunting round the roots of trees,
Today I returned home empty handed,
For a welcome cup of tea and toasted cheese.

In Praise Of Summer

Bathed in the golden rays of the sun,
My garden looks better,
With pretty perfumed roses,
In full bloom,
Than leaf empty trees,
And cold, clumsy fingers.

Give me days spent in shorts,
Happy memories of childhood pursuits,
Blackberrying with gran,
In quiet country lanes,
Hoping not to get bare arms scratched with thorns,
Fruit juice stained purple hands,
Then home to watch her make delicious jam.

Bathed in the golden rays of the sun,
Hours out on my bicycle,
Those seemingly never-ending days,
With laughing friends,
Lines filled with washing,
Birds singing their Midsummer melody,
Warm, light evenings after school,
Enjoying the playground of nature.

Divided By Time

Divided by time,
Distance,
City borders,
The night song trills in my ears,
No matter the miles between us.

My heart is yours to claim and keep,
In my waking hour when you're in deep sleep,
The time zones,
Days grumbles and groans,
No worries,
No cares.

The bright capitol city lights stare back at me,
Outlining the buildings I hold so dear,
Fair winds and faint breezes carry my laughter,
My love to you,
As the sunrises and sets,
Turns it's face to you,
My darkening hours turn yours to light.

I Go Back - inspired by Andreas

I go back to moth-coloured grey concrete flats,
Rooms where no sunlight ever penetrates,
Boarded up windows,
Metal shutters at each level.

On the stone steps the addicts gather,
Wild eyed and abusive,
Waving dirty finger nailed hands,
In rude gestures,
As I pick my way over denim covered skinny legs,
The lifts broken again,
As it's used as a urinal and vomiting booth,
I'm better off using the stairs.

I try not to step on part empty cans and bottles,
Stained spoons and screwed up foil,
Discarded syringes,
That it's come to this.

Sometimes I wish I could send down a basket,
On a rope to be filled with groceries,
Abseil off the roof to avoid them,
The women are the worst in their skimpy outfits,
Bodies sold so many times,
Semi-comatose and unashamed,
Displaying tattooed midriffs,
Piercings in lips and noses,
I shiver, but they are impervious to the cold.

Walking With Seth

Touching, moving, slow escaping,
Green water ripples patterning rocks,
Still air,
Musty smell of bracken,
Uncurling, feathered fronds,
By the river,
Stepping stones moss damp, slippery,
I hesitate, turn back,
My dog Seth, his lead restricting play,
Nose down, sniffing, pawing,
Today the water is cold,
But still inviting,
He looks for my approval,
I bend to stroke his solemn head,
Brown eyes pleading,
Unheeded,
With a whistle we return home.

How Vast

How vast a space,
Once a field of green,
Is now an ocean of blood red,
Termination of life,
In my dreams,
Germination of hope.

I see the beauty,
Of what will be again,
When the battle is over,
When the birds return,
To sing sweet songs of Springtime,
And dew will lie undisturbed on new growth.

I Stand At The Window

I stand at the window gazing out,
Is that a flutter of red silk?
My imagination?
Or are you really there?
My mind plays tricks,
As I so long for you to be near,
Look into those once warm eyes,
A smile never far from your lips.

In my mind's eye you are forever tending the
roses,
Old wicker basket on the ground,
You repaired its broken handle with string,
"It'll see me out," you said.

Half bent, secateurs in hand,
I can almost hear the snip, snip,
So many times I watched as decaying petals fell,
To land outside the basket,
You would turn with a wistful smile,
Retrieve the fading blooms.

We would sit on summer evenings,
Not talking,
Listening to the birds singing,
Beneath the honeysuckle archway,
Until twilight,
Our silence a joyous experience,
A contemplative togetherness,
Sometimes I would close my eyes and drift.

Now every warm evening I put out two garden
chairs,
Close my eyes and hope,
I live in make believe,
A pretend world until twilight,
I listen to the blackbird sing his pretty melody,
Sometimes, if I wait long enough,
For one fleeting moment,
I swear I smell your aftershave,

Hear your laughter.

Shadows From The Past

Shadows from the past travel before my eyes,
Memories of childhood,
How time flies,
Did birds really sing more sweetly
in the gardens of my youth?
When the sun always seemed to shine,
Is it just burnished truth?

Were the days really longer?
Before grey strands crept through my hair,
Was imagination keener?
Has age dimmed my eye?
Everywhere seemed cleaner,
Before the years sped by.

Where's the beaming little girl gone?
She fills the photo albums with her grin,
A spoiled grandchild,
I was the only one,
And the young girl posing with her dollies?
She's still somewhere deep within.

Love's Old Song

Love's old song plays a tuneful melody,
It's never out of fashion,
Though it's rhythm may change tempo,
From youth's heavy rock pulsating passion,
To the lullaby of advanced age.

Sometimes the notes surprise,
It's not always wise,
To trust the fickle fortissimo,
It may change without warning,
To become a jazz saxophone lament.

Instead of listening to the whole concerto,
We rushed headlong into romance in the first few
bars,
Only to regret later,
When I heard the orchestra play the overture of
betrayal.

Let me rest awhile dangling my fingers,
In the icy cold water of a requim mass,
I hoped for the Wedding March and the Hallelujah
Chorus,
At the very least the crotchets and quavers.
Of a smooth sounding ballad.

Limited

Limited by my own body,
Unable to walk or stand,
I need the care of others to get me through,
I dream of the days of youth,
Now I'm helpless,
Unwanted,
Cast aside,
Bad news,
My family say I'm a burden,
A problem to be solved,
I hear their whispers,
I'm a drain on their inheritance,
A thorn in their side.

Top Of The Morning To You

Top of the morning to you,
As I pick up my brushes and paint,
I'm here to create a masterpiece,
Sorry I'm a bit late,
Genius has no time sheet,
It doesn't clock off and on,
It's there in the blink of an eye,
Doesn't rely on WiFi,
To fill up the empty page.

Words are my passion,
My tools of the trade,
I can fall on my sword,
If I feel you are bored,
I can write in rhythm and rhyme,
Make you laugh with a witty line,
A sonnet Shakespearian in style,
May not raise much of a smile,
My odes may fall flat on the ground,
Perhaps you'll find this panegyric more profound.

Iambic metre, stanza, quatrain,
A couplet, a doublet, love's bittersweet refrain,
If I want to make you cry,
I can pluck sentimental soliloquy from the sky.

From Church Pew

Incantation, veneration,
Bend, kneel and pray,
Genuflections, crucifixion,
Religious icons on display.

From church pew,
The chosen few,
The dedicated and brave,
Line up in rows,
To take the silver chalice from the clergyman,
Who stands in the chancel,
While they file past In the nave.

United as one body,
Joined at the hip,
One by one take a sip,
From the blood and body of Christ.

Glass And Silk

Compare the look of glass and silk,
Soft shimmer sheen against the hard pane,
Warp and weft,
The sunlit days, hours of darkness,
On the right a door marked entrance,
Exit is on the left.

I turn my face against the patchy yellow light,
So few the days that snake into the distance,
So many the days that trail behind,
Wasted, so much untasted,
So many regrets,
Wrong paths chosen,
More lows than highs,
No burning passion, love made me frozen.

How can this list of dismal failure?
Be my life story,
I never sought fame and glory,
But this?
A volume of sparse pages,
Not much more than a chapbook,
Dull reading as any bystander,
Wouldn't take a second glance at my
autobiography,
Even friends would have to fake polite interest,
In the truth that stares back at me.

A Raspberry Ripple Sky

Beneath a raspberry ripple swirling sky,
I remember the delight,
Of early morning mist in London,
Dew on yesterday's newly mown grass,
As we ran bare footed, laughing,
Avoiding the cracks in the moss-edged slabs.

Peeping out at us the promise of sunshine,
At the dawn of a brand new day,
Summer smells already heady in the air,
Flowers opening ready for bees,
Gran's parasol and folded deckchair,
Away from our parents,
We could enjoy life, do as we pleased.

The Dream

When do I forget the dream?
I spun, wove over time,
To join the myriad heaps of long forgotten days,
Discarded when ill-health and old age,
Cast their frailties over my golden ideologies,
My carefully crafted hopes for the milestones in
life,
That most other people seem to enjoy,
While some of us struggle,
Never realise our potential,
Our rainbow never brightens up a dreary sky,
Our silver lining moments never arrive.

As I sit endless hours in nursing home armchair,
I wish I'd sold all my belongings,
Travelled the world,
Climbed a mountain,
Sailed into New York harbour,
Danced on Broadway,
But the dice have rolled against me,
Too soon I cry,
As Mr. De'ath points his crooked finger,
At the sign that says too late.

Christmas A Century Apart

Cold Christmas,
The bells sound flat,
Hungry faces at the table,
No fire or welcome mat,
Our family disjointed and forlorn,
Waiting for granny this bleak Christmas morn.

If it wasn't for the neighbours,
We would have no Christmas dinner,
Our mother about to give birth yet again,
Exhausted, old before her time,
The workhouse looms ever closer,
Since our father was killed on the front line.

Cold Christmas,
The bells sound flat,
No TV to watch,
Our dad saw to that,
Sold it for drugs money and booze,
Says there's nothing for him but use.

If it wasn't for the food bank,
We would have no Christmas dinner,
Served up by gran,
As our mum's back in prison.

My Jubilant Return

This is my jubilant return,
I am reborn today,
At my age it's my long awaited London debut,
The West End stage has beckoned me,
Caused a fire to burn within my heart,
A metamorphosis has taken place,
That old me,
Lies already forgotten among the gravestones,
For the coat of confidence fits at last,
See its golden shimmer catch the sunlight,
In the footlights I'm a star,
Instead of being lonely in a corner, out of sight,
I'm centre stage,
My voice bell-like,
I'm on fire,
My timing is perfect,
I remember every line,
This is my chance,
My name's up on Shaftesbury Avenue in lights.

Lamplight

Lamplight dim, night is falling,
Turn down the wick,
Smell of oil burning,
Horse's hooves on cobbles clatter,
Street vendors calls,
Housewives' mumbled doorstep chatter.

From the parlour window,
Damp, fire unlit,
I watch the men, almost invisible,
Coal dust covered,
Weave home from the pit,
Where many nights I've stood and waited,
To walk home excitedly with dad.

Now he lies,
My silent companion,
As cold as the marble hearth,
In the shadow of the black diamond,
That claimed his life,
Tomorrow pa will descend for the last time,
Into the frozen, unwelcoming earth.

We Stand Here Together

We stand here together,
United as one voice,
Calling out for peace from the wilderness,
Looking down onto a world in such a mess,
Billions of pounds spent every year on defence,
Where's the sense?

We're wasting our resources,
Destroying planet earth,
Millions are starving,
But life's cheap,
Do those people really have any worth?
Out there beyond the horizon,
A land in life we'll never see,
But for those of us who believe,
It will be home for all eternity.

One day we'll have to answer for our
misdemeanours,
Why we allowed folk to die in misery,
Watched babies born without the opportunity,
To grow and thrive,
Don't get us started on the subject of abortion,
It's murder dressed up in a technical name,
Have we no conscience?
Have we no shame?
Are our hearts as hard as stone?
Do we stand on the sidelines?
Are we as bad?
Do we condone?
Violence,
Aggression,
Abuse,
Our world is so beautiful,
Yet we continue to misuse,
Creation,
Destroy the rainforest,
Justify our financial greed,
With platitudes and lies.

So our animals one by one become extinct,
We've used up our only chance,
The two by two olive branch,
Ponder this,
Somewhere a poor child is taking its last breath,
You can cheat on your partner,
Cheat the tax man,
But no matter what you do,
You can't cheat death.

Made in the USA
Charleston, SC
17 August 2016